It
Happened
Within
the
Sun

Sun Queen

Book Cover, Editing, and Interior Design by
Chell Reads Publishing
www.chellreads.com

Dedication

To my reflections, know all your dreams are worth making them come true. Remember the most natural thing in life to do is be you. Trust yourself lighten the world with your spirit.

Acknowledgements

I want to thank the Creator most of all because without the Creator I wouldn't have the gift of writing. I thank you for every blessing and obstacle.

I want to give thanks of gratitude to my family and friends. Thank you for believing in me whether I am fighting for justice or expressing myself through poetry. I want to express my most profound appreciation to all those who encouraged me to complete this book.

I want to thank my mother for her unconditional love and support; she has promoted me as if she was getting paid, lol. Mom, you're a beautiful soul. My brother, Tyrone Jr., thank you for always supporting me and believing you have the world's greatest sister because you do. When I told you, I was writing a book you were like "okay, so let's start a publishing company." I say that to say you always have back in any of my endeavors and I thank you. To My Dad, Tyrone Sr., I appreciate all of our ups and downs they have bridged us together and of course gave me things to write about.

My partner, Ashleigh Huckabey, thank you for being my first personal editor. I appreciate all of your support, advice, and motivation throughout this new book writing process with me. I can't thank you enough for brainstorming along side me no matter the hour. I would also like to thank you for all the tea you made to help increase my creativity.

My editor, Michelle Morrow, thank you for providing me with high energy; for assisting me with more than punctuation and grammatical errors. Through this process, you reminded me of how worth it, in the end, it would be, and I am grateful for your services.

To the Late Elizabeth L. Fain and the Late Christopher Fain, I love you both so much and miss you dearly. I hope I am making both of you proud. Energy never dies, so I thank you both for journeying with me. When we meet, I will have signed copies for you, my Beloved Grandmother and brother.

Contents

Dear Reader,

Thank you for feeling inclined to read my book. I thank you for journeying with me. I am grateful you allowed my artistic narrative into your life. May, It Happened Within the Sun bring some source of empowerment. I write to bring light to my darkness to get a better understanding of both elements. While reading, I wish to inspire you to get intimate with your true self. I pray you will have courage and clarity along your journey.

I encourage you to examine your true self to keep trying until you are satisfied; everyone deserves peace and freedom. There has probably been a time of many you felt like there was no one who understood you. You may have felt on different occasions the person was not listening to you. Or a time when you didn't know what you had a passion for in this thing, we all know as life or the matrix. When you take time to understand yourself questions are answered your soul sends messages to your brain. It's one of the most empowering things you can do.

If you feel you need help to answer questions know it's okay to seek help. One of the greatest gifts in life is presenting yourself with the understanding of your true self. Your true self wants to rescue you. If you ever had feelings of doubt and disappointment give yourself a chance to be your best self. You deserve it.

Overcoming struggles will be a part of the journey. The formula for overcoming struggles is to surrender your old self, all negative energy and environments. Set yourself free to attend to the things you have control of in your life. Who knows, you may be your own superhero. The effect of studying oneself is crucial to unleashing your higher self. It allows you to build an alliance with your consciousness and the person you were created to be. Love yourself you may not be where you want to be at this moment in your life. Be patient; you can always change lanes look both ways believe in yourself. Put your signal on and move forward. The power of change begins with you. Self-reflection is powerful. Trust yourself you will discover new energy that will awaken you.

Inspirational Quotes

Experience life as your whole self.

There's freedom within looking deeper than a mirror can see.

The key is not to speak about healing but to unlock the door to enter the healing room.

Your past scars are a part of a formula to help you further your future.

Break through your illusions experience life in honesty and truth.

Life changes so quickly you must learn from the light and heat from the Sun.

Peace comes from your light free yourself and shine.

Introduction

It happened within the Sun is a poetic compilation fueled by my thoughts, confessions, experiences, and truths. There was a knock on my head; the intensity in my awakening was growing stronger. I viewed the landscape of the universe differently. There was a time I would try to cut the pain. Now I meditate and cry with the purpose to help myself heal. Some of my work also captures conversations and encounters in my life. My poetry was a referee between me and my thoughts. There were times I wouldn't be able to pick myself out of a lineup. The activities in my head would cause nausea. Picture it being a dark matter and your eyes aren't closed, soft pillows and harsh thoughts.

I got the chance to fall in love through my pen. Through my work, you'll be able to see and feel the changes through the seasons and the road I took through my journey. It took my thoughts to calm down and for me to have a heart to heart with myself. I felt love, anger, power, inspiration, and disappointment. Things I didn't have answers so I would write so they could unfold. And I could speak it once I realized the purpose. Often, I had too many thoughts on my brain. I felt I couldn't digest. Writing gave me the chance to unscramble and rearrange my dreams to live or die. With words, it gave me the opportunity to start over again.

I gave my pen the authority to help me understand parts of myself and sections of my brain. To decipher what I wanted to manifest in the universe. Within the sun I once was lost, hurt, happy, trusting amongst so many other things. You know how your thoughts sometimes you can have wanting to jump in the ocean or rule the world. To be held captive by your thoughts, covers were thrown off of me. Imagine permission given to mind and body for sleepless nights. I knew my thoughts eventually would be the compass for my awakening. I could now see the spirals in nature informing me change was on the way.

Before we can understand someone else, we have to indulge in our SELF. Have a different mind to include accountability, an experienced clinician wouldn't know what to do with me until I first admitted to my problem. Thinking often scares me the tunes in my head sounds like a beginner drum player. Please don't leave me alone with my thoughts. Is what I wanted to say often but the words never left my head. I know my thoughts are reviewing my issues. The voices in my head analyze my pain. I yell, cry, kick and scream!! I'm scared, but without my thoughts I'm lonely. I want more prosperous ideas; I want to understand the concepts in my head. I'm getting frustrated by this battlefield. The voices in my head tell me not to quit, opening my heart and embracing my thoughts. Here are all levels of consciousness. I do not need to be diagnosed; I need to be my true self. My story reveals the responsibility of finding the truth and not walking through the roads of deception.

Part One: I am Art

Dear Sun

Balance and align with the Universe. Thanks for taking the time to acknowledge you will spend more time trusting in the energy from the Sun. To create a new space, a fresh perspective to walk by faith in Life's process. Thank you for allowing a restored vision, for seeing all is destined for you. While reading, I welcome you to find new energy including a firm balance. Having the heart to worship peace no matter what comes your way. The absolute truth is you are a phenomenal link to Earth and Sun. Realize your strength; you have the power to create intense energy.

There are many levels of consciousness. So, cheers to a diverse range of artistry navigating through life's journey; relax vibe with the imagery that will pour from my pen.

I love you Sun!

Numbers don't lie. And as I sit and think about some things I have been through. I can count all the dysfunction, pain, disparities, and fear. During that time, I had seen things as if they were out of my control —witness domestic violence, class

18

projects destroyed, house raided by the boys in blue. I just wanted the power to control things around me. Later in life, I realized life is what you make it. I never went without a meal I just been hungry since I was a little girl. My dreams kept their hands around me.

A self-revolution elegantly elevates your ego. It's a fire burning for you to find the solution to your issues. It has you speaking to yourself. Asking questions like what is my purpose here? What am I doing to change my plight? Are your dreams feeling like explosives blowing your mind? Your life changes in a significant way of meeting yourself. My rejuvenate soul signed a contract with the Universe for my rebirth. It was time for a broken spirit to heal. It is time to forgive and set myself free.

I will create peace in my Queendom. I will protect my energy. I will value my conscious I will protect my body. I will commit to balance and order I will act accordingly at all times because I am a Queen.

Self-Diagnosis

Seeing entails more than vision
I may look healthy, but I have a physical
deformity.
Diagnosed with pain, my facial expressions are
scared.
Looking in the mirror,
it appears to be a fractured posture with
ruptured self-esteem.
Everything is driving me insane.
Concentrating with so many problems on my
plate is hard.
Stressing can't be healthy
I can't eat until my issues become obsolete.
I declined help because I don't want to speak.
I adjusted to the pain and became comfortable
with the roadblocks.
I feel like a full-time employee of the
Pain Factory.

Sun Writes

I am the author of my story
My freedom of expression
Able to wake up my dream
To share what I've endured
Lifting my words subscribing to my pen
My pen brings alive my creative side
It explores my soul
My right and wrongs
Where I been and where I was going
I was able to see with my words
Through my pen, I am able to confess, compose,
imagine, and inspire
Writing was a gift I decided to manifest
From the ink to the stroke of my pen
To the sound, it makes striking the paper to the
releasing of words
It's all a part of my healing
Able to confess through my pen
Reveal my convictions and revolution
I trust my pen to write my testimony
I get amazed by words
Daily affirmations give me courage
It helps me prepare for battles
I can speak life and light through my pen
Take a stand in my shadows

21

Sun Queen

It was more effective than watching the blood
pour from my skin
I was safe and, in my comfort, zone writing
Sun writes to give a voice to her thoughts
Thanks, be unto my pen
Writing is an invitation to my journey through
words and expression
I am not alone
I have my words looking back at me
My struggle is also the source for my solution
When I don't understand words come to help me
to convey
My pen can be unpredictable
Overall, my pen has been good to me
Don't we live by our words?
Words can create a heaven or hell
Words are powerful
Writing allows you to add and subtract
I cried, died, panicked, and came alive through
my pen
There were times I felt like I was alone and
broken
I would write to come alive
To replay things in my mind
To meet the experience again
Maybe I would receive differently this time
Writing is meeting my match

It Happened Within the Sun

I have to challenge myself
Explain my viewpoints
Get to know the person that sounded like me
Keep writing through the test
Be real with my feelings
When I had no one to call
I would write
Declaring my faith in the rising of my
breakthrough.
My mother presented me with life that I may
grow and understand what it is like to live. She
produced the name Lauren Nicole for me. It was
the universe that prompted me to develop into
Sun Queen. In life, you can create what you want
and become who you desire. The change was
calling out to me, and I could not answer as the
same person. I knew I had a light within me that a
screenshot would not be able to capture. I can
remember times when I would hear why you
can't be more like her. Or my flaws/vices were
uplifted more than my genuine self. My light was
my protector in darkness, during the times I was
unsure of whom I was created to be. You ever
had rug burn due to being on your knees praying
that heartache be moved from your home; to let
Love enter and shake off the heavy load. I don't
want to know my name until I make things

change. Now things are coming full circle I feel balanced, I am now becoming an expert on serving myself.

Lauren to Sun

You have to be your closest friend
Everything was changing around me
I knew it was time to lead in the right direction
Righteousness was embedded in me; it was
evident
So apparently, I had to change with the time
I energized the soul
I let shit go and became Sun
Put pieces together, sobered up, and lifted myself
from the darkness
Told myself the truth
I needed to see myself in a higher place
Opened my mind and became wise
I took chances agreeing to disagree with the
moods
Challenged my thoughts
Eager to see what was on the other side
To find the positive in any circumstance
Live with no regrets; no self-judgments
Knowing I was the prize
Elevating pass the sky
See I already been around the solar system
In the midst of it, all the Sun cured me
So, I became Sun
It sheltered me with an enormous, hot mass of
brightness

Sun Queen

I deserved it all
It shocked a new wave within me
Had me thinking all natural with a powerful
turbulence
The old me was a memory decayed
My authentic self was worth fighting for
I am inspired by energy
I release light and gravitate to souls
I am available to my head and heart
I had to rise
Transcending my dreams with the Reality that I
am the Sun
A blessed Queen
It made sense to find my identity
My place in the world
I found confirmation; I had to free my mind
Warm the waves with a lifetime of Love and
energy
The rest of the stars depended on me
I am Sun
A cold world but I'm committed to self-awareness
An internal breakthrough within woke me up
High beans flashed inside me
I sacrificed myself for the rebirth of my higher self
Don't I deserve to live as a masterpiece?
A colorful, complex, and dimensional picture
Organic and genuine

It Happened Within the Sun

Made with a magical brush
It feels so good to see through clear lenses
I hold special powers, so it was time to connect
and manifest
I owed it to myself to learn more about my true
self.
To grow in my revolutionary ideologies
Hey,
It's okay to invade yourself
There's Power in my name
Self-revolution elevates your ego in a gracious
way
It's a fire burning for you to find the solution to
your issues
It has you speaking to yourself answering back
No, I'm not crazy
Who has the answers beside me?
I had to find myself and begin changing my plight
Learning me was explosive
This journey has blown my mind
I'm not finished yet
Giving myself the green light to go
To not live in society's box
I am the author of my story
I created a new narrative
I appreciate everything I been through
Now I know I am the Sun

Sun Queen

In sync with the Universe
I shine
I am Sun

Attracted to Self

The change in the universe begins within you. Find your way through the hole located in your ozone layer. It doesn't necessarily take a degree to accomplish your goals or a diamond to bring you to the altar of life. I hope you paid attention to the lessons in school and life. It's no mystery lessons don't just happen within an institution. Tools and techniques to survive can come from the streets or a stranger. Development can come from your demons if you identify the sources that will support you in your change process, you will realize all components will help to balance you. Can you feel the shift? Do you hear the echo of your greater self? Take a minute to give thanks to the good, bad and indifferent they all serve a purpose. Don't be distant from yourself have a conversation with yourself and realize you are a radical substance.

You ever get wrapped up in nature talking to the birds? Taking your shoes off to vibe with the grass and sun gaze or noticing the sweet melody from the blowing of the wind. Take a day to be one with nature. Let nature be the music your soul needs.

There is no need to hide from the world push through you will make it.

I am the Earth

I am Magic

I am Science

I am Nature

The laws of attraction and nature reside within me. I am open to life and its conditions. It all starts in my mind. I take time to reflect on the experiences happening in my galaxy.

Study Thy Self

We often get lost looking for answers.
Gettin' scared not knowing if we are heading in
the correct direction.
We underestimate our characteristic that plays a
role in our diverse population.
Not identifying and building on our differences.
There's no course that outlines life.
The classes are the daily strides and peddling
through the struggles of Life.
The daily challenges of living in a distorted society
and having motivation is vital.
It helps you to rise above the heartbreaks, adapt
when needed.
Empowering yourself to understand your roots.
Reflect
Construct a new policy, so your individuality is a
part of the curriculum.
You do not have to wait long to explore your
personality and figure out reality.
Love yourself search within for additional
sources.
Love yourself endlessly.
Who you are contributing to the make-up of
society?

Maintenance of Self

Self-Efficacy is more than a chore; it must be
instilled within me
My emotional experiences helped me to explore
the TRUE
concept of Me
I had to identify my fear
I addressed being in denial
Before suicidal thoughts digested in my mind
I discovered logical life paradigms to assist with
managing my traumatic events
I embraced the diversity that's incorporated in
me
I looked forward to accomplishing my dreams
Becoming knowledgeable of all that I've seen,
things I've done, my stressors that caused pain
Creating an atmosphere that describes me!
Thanks for being a part of my constellation

Self-Crushing

I had to save my soul
That required me to get naked
Taste my own juices
Pull the mask off
Switch the music in my head
Spin on my sorrow
Trash the self-torment
Curve the criticism of self
Submit to self
Bring out my creative side
Broaden myself within my culture
Who am I anyway?
What's my purpose?
What's going to keep me going?
Before staring at my soul
I had to break bread with my mind and body
I couldn't take any sick days or FMLA
I had to address adversity
Love myself more
Know my worth and dedicate my days to
removing
the dirt of my brain

Part Two: Echoes

Sunlight

The sun flows with you in every beat and stroke
You are an artistic melody
Be appreciative of who you are
You're a star
Restock your elevation
Let everyday bring new hope
Truth in your direction
Why be a tourist in your world
Let every day and the days to follow speak to you
Today and the days to follow you will respond
with gratitude and integrity
Take the veil off, allow yourself to see and feel
Green Light!
Step into your awakening
I hope you find out who you are
Stand your ground you belong to the original
people
You are not a black tourist in a white universe
Don't let your existence get caught up in a racist
guide in your journey
Take advantage of your melanin and freedom.
You embody royalty
There are no flaws in your complexion
They won't give you back what they stole
May your conscious be activated by your truth
and the love you have for yourself

Sun Queen

You are not a mistakes or misunderstanding
Don't let anyone prosecute you for your being

Why Am I Black?

Why did you make me Black?
Amerikkka will have you thinking like
The boys in blue aren't here to protect me or you
Your womb will be violated, and it's okay
Be silent because no one will believe you
You know why?
Because you're black
Why did you make me Black?
They want my skin in the background
Most of the days underneath the ground
I can't lead because of the color of my skin
All eyes on me
Funny thing is I'm invisible in society
I get checked in the airport differently
All I'm trying to do is catch a flight
Then again, my skin is black how far can I get in
the world of white supremacy, oppression,
injustice, and no transparency?
What in the world is going on?
Is it because you made me Black?
Did you mean to create my life?
Do you want it back?
Walls surrounding me planted sturdy all around
me
The bricks can't be moved even if you tried
If the walls could talk, they'd probably ask,

Sun Queen

Why did you make her Black?
Financial wealth doesn't seem like it will come my
way
System plotting against me
Catching cases because of the color of my skin
Would it had been better if you made me in a
different image
A lighter pigment
Society isn't good tome
Tears in my eyes from the dehumanizing
What did you do to me?
I'm not free
Why did you make me Black?
Suffering
Am I the enemy?
Is it because I'm Black?
They fear my melanin
They try to take me out every chance they get
Harass me in the streets
Flashlight in my face
Asking for ID
Standing outside aggravated pressed up against
the white fence
Am I being charged?
What did I do?
Or you pulled me over because you see me living
while black

It Happened Within the Sun

Because I'm black, I can be killed for a broken tail
light or
Murdered with my hands up
You heard me ask for you not to shoot my hands
were up
Damn!
No due process
All because of the color of my skin
Don't all people deserve a second chance?
Not me though because I'm Black
I deserve no praise
Because I'm the color of dirt
Next thing you know people will walk around
with a R. I. P shirt
Why did you make me black? It's not acceptable
My blackness makes me a savage and a thief
My human rights don't exist because of the color
my skin
I'm a black girl they expect my dreams to die
To go through life being loud with a bad attitude
Placed in a community with overflowing liquor
stores
Abandoned buildings
Told the highest I can go is the ceilings of the
prison
Here I am black
There's a war on me

Sun Queen

Save me from the color of my skin
Black Girl, (Black Women)
Understand this
You were made you Black because you are
Powerful
You are Black without apology
You have a connection with the Earth
You are the closest to the Sun
You are magnificent
You are magical
There isn't anything that you will let break you
Everything thrown in your path will strengthen
you
You are truth, wisdom, and light
Shine Black Girl
Shine Black Women
I made you Black because you are art
You are life
No one grinds like you
No one is resilient like you
Black girl (Black Women)
You can start a fire and put it out
You are a first aid kit
You save lives
What other being has strong shoulders like you?
You are A Deity/Goddess/ Empress /Queen
Why did I make you Black?

It Happened Within the Sun

I made you Black for the world to get baptized in
your frequencies.
You enlightened soul
Do you taste your freedom?
Rise Black girl (Black woman)
Save the world
Because the world needs you

Speak Up and Within

Oh, Magical Creator of the Universe,
The source of love and life
Invest in me
I come to you for clarity on this divide
Save me from myself
I appreciate all you have set in front of me even
my sides
The bottom isn't for me
I'm a walking testimony
During meditations I listen and wait for a sign
Thoughts dance in my mind
The moves tell their own story
I think, rethink, and think again
I'm waiting
I'm trying to transcend past the environment of
the stories relayed through the media
The lack of data found in these out-of-date books
Take me to Kemet
I'm ready to explode
Disrupt anything that isn't for the betterment of
me
I am everything to me
I know I can be my own savior
My history/her story present with seeds
I receive signals through the trees

It Happened Within the Sun

For its roots sends messages to the universe to
reach me
That I may properly understand
In a spiritual way
May the ancestors be with me as I take steps
through this journey
I am not here to assume
But merely expand my resume
Examine the sun and sand
The universal law of what's going on
To be fortunate before it's all said and done
Weights can't hold me down
I want to taste, feel, and smell the fruits of my
labor
I am the chosen one
Fight through the pollution, brutality, and
corruption
To stand for the unfortunate ones who are a part
of mass incarceration
Let me be a solid rock
To feed the hunger cries
To shine and align with my sovereign self
I will not short change myself
I will not have an enslaved mentality
Let me lean on you
Magical creator don't move I need you
Heads shots

Sun Queen

Mental wounds
I don't see myself in ICU or in the ground
Fighting to stay alive
Mend a broken brain
Sometimes you have to deliver yourself from
yourself
It's up to me to make it right
There's no room for me in shadows
Protecting me is a must
I have to maintain and stay sane
There's no entrance for the opposition
All my chakras have to get on the same page
I can't mentally die
Or be in prison within my brain
Imagine being in the middle of negativity and
positivity
It's a new marketplace
I no longer want to feel the pain
Be at war with myself
Time to make adjustments
So, I'm here yearning power
The Goddess in the mirror told me I was a walking
trophy
This isn't a play
It's my personal Revolution
It's time to ascend
To wrap myself up in peace

It Happened Within the Sun

I'm outgrowing the old me
Higher vibrations is calling me
I want to be filled up with warm joy
Open up my third eye
It's time to take action and be there for me
There's no one to blame or cover up from
I'm here to be present in my true self
Reveal the sweetness in my rhythm
To allow my higher self to greet me
Discover new strengths
Show my gratitude for change
This is my blessing to wake up
Beauty
To learn my ultimate purpose and take
responsibility for the way I live.
The guidance is in my heart
The investment in me doesn't lose its value
I can't ever be broke; if I be myself
I will reject the negative spirits
Shake all uncertainty
I will evolve and over stand
There's evidence in my DNA to support my claim
I'm no superhero
A divine being
Ain't no giving up
All my manifestations will come true
There's a brighter side to the struggle

Sun Queen

So, I'm rearranging my thoughts
Suiting up to walk in my truth
Change is on the way
No more standing around
In a place of despair
It isn't too late to write a new chapter
My strength and passion is intense
I'm approaching this with all my limbs
My chin above the waters
Soon I'll be standing on the highest mountain
Fist up to the sky
I will be patient and trust the process
I'm here to receive all that is mine
Put in all the time to be amazed with my self-
discovery
I trust myself to win
This is the season for Self-Understanding
I speak into the Universe the evolution of me
It's what I declare
To be the Light and love of my life
You've discovered the importance of your
struggle.
You took time to learn from your mistakes
disassociating from cycles.
The distance to success isn't far at all
You're on a path to helping yourself transform.

Practice patience you will discover the
importance of your life's experiences.
Relax!
Find balance.
I Love you!

Appreciate the Struggle

With being disconnected you'll never understand
the meaning of Peace, Unconditional Love does
exist
Sunshine comes from the inside
Commit to healing you; there's value in knowing
you
You may not see it, but your struggle provides
strength
Analyze things fully through
Comfort your emptiness
There's no need to be insecure
Demonstrate the urge of educating yourself
Pain and adversity are circumstances that do not
stop us from elevating
Circumstances and situations do not stay nor
define you
The universe contains perfections and endorses
imperfection to work for the Greater Good
There's nowhere to hide don't become a prisoner
to your Mind
Running will not benefit in restoring you
Connect with yourself; find your light
Smile and accept your tears
Let fear be memory
A stress storm cannot live in the center of you

It Happened Within the Sun

Lessons are beautiful
Be still form a relationship with getting to know
you
Don't cheat yourself
Love Yourself
Accept your spiritual energy
Ditch the negative mentality
Journeying through this thing we know as Life
We always question why
Nothing beats a Failure but a Try
Knowing nothing is guaranteed
On a quest searching for balance
Unclog your mind engage with the waves
You are an expert on this Ride
Your struggle will guide you to your Destiny
March into a Happier and Healthier You
Look back to where you've come from
You have discovered the importance of your
struggle
The distance to Self-Awareness and Success isn't
quite far
Practice patience you will discover the
importance of your life experience
Kissed by Self Discovery
Tune in and Relax
Appreciate Your Struggle

Vibrate

Don't cheat yourself: Love Yourself
Accept your spiritual energy
Ditch the negative mentality
Journeying through this thing we know as Life
We always question why
Make a commitment to rise up and improve
yourself
You are an expert on this Ride
Hurting Inside
It's interrupting what the creator has in store for
me
The rage has me acting a fool, hurting my
brothers and sisters
I'm at war with my own fist
Looking in the mirror asking for me
From the dysfunction of the systemic way and the
black cloud over my city
I hide in my True Self
Afraid to admit
I don't know me, I want to be loved and
understood
I barely recognize what family is
Haven't been to a reunion in a minute
I don't know the last time my immediate family
sat down together at dinner time

It Happened Within the Sun

Shit when the sun rises
I can't relate to the sunshine
And the kid down the block probably went to bed
hungry
The girl around, I'm sure was touched her uncle
again
My language is blood
I keep my thoughts inside because I don't want
any pity
I know I have to release my feelings though
So here I am shedding some of these feelings
A couple of verses to help you think twice
There's no safe place to hide when you're trying
to live
I want somebody to have my back
It's been a cold season that extends throughout
my historical timeline
Amerikkka guilty for the enslavement of my
ancestors, not respecting our humanity
The civil servants in blue communicating with us
uncivilized actions
Flashing lights
Screaming disputes
Being slaughtered because of our Melanin
Tears tattooed on the walls of my people's death
chambers
Flint without water is a form of depopulation

Sun Queen

But what do I know?
To a degree, I believe in conspiracy theories
Today's living is parallel to Jim Crow
We need to get in sync with our higher selves
Stop hustling backward
Thinking peace is foreign
I get it; it scares us to admit and disclose our
trauma
Figuring we'll always be a Nigga
We walk the Earth with so much pain in our
hearts
The youth feeling alive and empowered because
they have access to carry a gun on their hip
Not thinking they're special enough to invent
something
To live their dreams
Throwing their hands up when they get frustrated
with a math problem
Mama barely home to help resolve problems
She's working two and three jobs to avoid the
eviction and disconnected notices
Decision-making skills aren't the hot topic on the
block
See you have to understand in some homes
Kids are raising themselves and siblings and
teaching their parents things

It Happened Within the Sun

Oh, didn't I mention how the system tries to
leave the Black man out our homes
Yea so not too many Fathers in the home on my
block
I must get rid of these generational scars
I believe I can change the world that's why I had
to grab my pen
And cry on my note pad
I got to release this mental slavery
The Revolution starts within me
I will not be a part of a timeline where reflecting
on life is an affliction of lies and False
opportunities
These dark times can change
Shit, I no longer have to visit my dad behind bars
These days have been feeling strange
We must get it right
Understand the power of our His/Her story
America's language appears to be hate.
Here we are in the 21st Century still fighting and
resisting white Supremacy, Bigotry, and the
Klansman.
An era of Stop and frisk; talk of bordering walls.

Sun Queen

Doomed Spirits
Life is one grand mystery
Struggling to find purpose in a complex society
Human behavior detached from emotions
We are familiar with vague and tainted
responses, drug quantity in the streets total more
than ounces
People in office neglecting accountability
How do I vote for thee?
Bruised from over 400 years of slavery
Nightmares because of Fear
Just wanting to be Free
Being told you're not good enough
Blinded by their history
Reached out to be rescued
Passed by; beaten away from the light
Who's responsible for people's lack of identity?
A black sheep on land your forefathers created
Racism a cloud that hangs over all galaxies
There are unexplained behaviors, senseless
murders, and undiagnosed disorders
A cold life
Discrimination and Disconnect all in my face
Beyond sad and blue
Until the end of time
I'm fighting to the World is Mine

I'm fighting for a better world where they don't
believe I belong
But who am I?

I live in a city where it feels like the Police
Department wants me to be paralyzed. No news
regarding my brother's case. The mayor appears
to get involved in only certain cases and helping
certain families. Involvement and Engagement
always appear differently around election time,
etc. I am not sure if my city has a special homicide
rubric. Missing my brother is an understatement.
I will forever be grateful for his short time here
on earth. For his flesh is gone but our memories
are everlasting especially, his warming smile. His
life was cut short; he did not get to accomplish all
he wished to do or fully develop. I hope looking
over our family feels like an accomplishment for
as he gets to sit high and is now our angel. I feel
your presence for your energy will never die.
Shine Bright for I will always know which star you
are!

Sun Queen

Somewhere a little girl has been hurt and trampled on. Her dollhouse collapsed, she's sad. Her childhood stripped, her privacy invaded. She doesn't want to go and play. Somewhere a young lady was caught in crossfire. She's lying somewhere wrapped in bandages. Through the bandages you see her tatted tears. She's not breathing on her own hooked up to so many tubes. She's holding on reflecting on her life. She takes one last breath, remembering she has no support.

#MeTOO

Me too is more than a hashtag
It's the nightmare inside many girls and women's
minds
The monster(s) that penetrated their minds with
the scary things
How do I believe in anything?
I didn't believe in the treatment I received
I was robbed
Manhandled and told to lay right there
To be still
I didn't want it in my dreams or reality
I couldn't tell if I was for sale or not
How much were the tickets?
Was he doing this to make a dollar?
I'm young; this is overwhelming
Why is this old man in my room taking off his
pants?
Telling me to hush and never say anything
because no one would ever believe me.
In that very moment my life ended
There was no joy; I just wanted to play with my
toys
I was powerless raped of my freedom
Fuck the birds and the bees this shit compares to
being hung from a tree
Crucified for having a vagina

Sun Queen

I wanted my pillow to save me or end me
An unhealthy mind at the age of 9
Wanting to run away from home
Leaving my body home
Is there a way I can start over?
He stole my prize; my womb
Shit I wish I never made an exit out of Mommas
womb
I was his sex slave at a young age
Who gave him permission to disrupt my
development?
I could barely tell time
But I know this was not right in any moment or
time
Stained sheets from Uncle Rick experimenting
with me at the age of 9 with my pre-mature
hormones
Often times, I wondered if he was intoxicated
I would look up at the door waiting for sobriety to
walk through
My mama or someone
This tragedy was another trigger for me to
withdraw from the world and myself
Hating the skin, I was in,
Touched by him
Sleepless nights and fragile bones
Corrupted by strokes of a man I thought was Kin

It Happened Within the Sun

Releasing his loads of saliva and erection inside
me
Who's to blame for this behavior?
Is it me?
This can't be expected of me
What am I burnt offerings?
More went on inside my walls than inside my
childish mind
His hands were so big they would wrap around
my throat
I would close my eyes hoping I could do a magic
trick and disappear
I couldn't breathe
I just remember my body being twisted
He couldn't have paid attention to my pig tails
I'm a kid Mister
Get off Me
But I couldn't breathe I was frozen in my tears
How will I ever appreciate me?
Look what's happening to me
I wish I could express the boundaries crossed
Again, I can't breathe
There's a big long object being forced in me
I don't remember this being in the fairytales I
read
This couldn't be the response from the stars I
looked at

Sun Queen

and prayed upon
I should've been playing with my dolls
Instead, there were so many bloody tears I
shared with the moon
I would stare out the window waiting and wishing
someone would burn down this room
To release me from this toxic home
When I tried to tell mom, she yelled and sent me
back to my room without comfort
Fuck!
Then Uncle Rick becomes my baby sitter
Now, I have a permanent shiver in my voice
Left alone to not breathe
I'm only 9 I want to talk
#StopTheSilence

Part Three: Blood Stone

A Broken Dream in Amerikkka

WTF is The Amerikkkan Dream?
Repenting to a white man to set you free
Asking for Mercy
Paid my tithes and can't get a seat or help from
the congregation
We live in a world of sinmental
Things are unbelievable and unjust
And if good and bad didn't exist we wouldn't be
able to comprehend balance
Not because of a bite from an apple
The glory of Self may bring light to your Dream
Or maybe not the dream Amerikkka seems to
have is the death on us
Sallie Mae, in debt from college tuition
The institution they thought I would never make
it to because I was raised in the hood
White supremacy always unraveling
Corruption from the government has citizens
falling for anything
Swiping into the Oppressors gate
Opportunities in the industry if eye bleach my
skin
Amerikkka
The homeless person who sleeps in a tent?

It Happened Within the Sun

Look around you there are people on the streets
sleeping in tents
The brutality done to my reflections has me
traumatized
Here I am trying to get a job at the bank and I
never learned about savings and investments at
home
People being taken to jail due to child support or
marijuana they sold to put money in my seed
piggy bank?
Because of the Stigma on Mental Health
A few receiving help
Hung because of our skin pigment
Homicides Unit act have free time
Chris, Quayvon and Dae Dae murders go unsolved

Debt in America

What is the American Dream?
What does Democracy look like?
Is democracy alive or dead?
When you think education will bring so much
pleasure and success.
Remember hearing education will make your
dreams come true.
So, you became in love with gaining knowledge
Embarking on new things and experiences that
will enlarge your stability
But debt wrapped its arms all around me.
I told myself I wouldn't be a statistic.
I was going to earn a degree, and it was going to
help me out the hood.
I had to take care of Mama.
I knew I had to explore and see what doors
education opened.
But nothing is guaranteed.
So, you wake up to The Student Loan Department
on your line.
Morning voice
I want to be like Lauren isn't available.
Matter of fact this isn't her phone.
Don't call back!
When you find her tell her I said Hi!

It Happened Within the Sun

Ugh
How did they get my number?
Oh, yea! Remember, you enrolled in college?
At the moment you are no longer happy about
your studies.
Yes,
Hello,
I can't afford to pay these loans back.
Next,
Wishful thinking
Feelings of slumber
Here I am trying to pay bills on time
Working 80hrs plus overtime.
Why does it feel like I'm working to earn pennies,
nickels, and dimes?
Why isn't education free?
This isn't fair!
The government makes a fee or three for
everything.
How much is this air?
Oh, respiratory conditions and health problems.
America tells you go get an education.
And leave out the fine print.
The system isn't focused on me.
Is this a setup?
Where was the insert about a lifetime agreement
being in debt?

Sun Queen

I couldn't give up
To sustain day to day in life did I really need a degree?
Receiving mail and calls are constant replays.
I need to eat, live, and maintain
Did I mention I would love to travel?
I can't escape the system.
All this schooling has to pay off.
Speak it into existence.
You will be debt free.
Mr. Sam
Mr. Tom
FICA
Government
Do you want to trade?
You can take this degree back.
The education quotes and slogans in my ear I don't know.
Not sure I will get to see or feel what the good life is like.
This brown skin is up against so many isms.
Way too many excuses over qualified and under qualified stories.
Not enough experience.
What if I don't land the career I planned?
This can't be real life!
Picture it

It Happened Within the Sun

The recession we always talked about.
What's the currency of education?
Maybe I should've enrolled in the Army/Navy
something.
Ha!
Who am I kidding; who was fighting in a war?
I have my own war going on.
I have an issue with the system.
It tries to keep my melanin in bondage.
Nor do I wish to feel like a minority on the land
my ancestors prepared.
I shouldn't fear a position because I'm a Black
woman.
Or worry about the lack of paid leave when it's
time to give labor.
And my locks fall to the middle of my back.
I have so many questions the school system
didn't supply enough
information on financial literacy.
I wasn't too impressed with the history in the
textbooks either.
The same ole stories about Dr. King.
Leaving out so many fundamental facts
And leaving out thousands of black leaders and
investors.
Just frustrated!
I had to pass statistics

Sun Queen

But who told me buying groceries and packing a
lunch would be hard.
Of course, I make too much for government
assistance.
Who made up all these guidelines, anyway?
They told me I could conquer the world.
Did that include robbing Peter to pay Paul?
I try to be particular about the heat in the winter
and air in the summer.
A check doesn't last a lifetime.
Neither does debt.
Remove me from your call log and system.
Take back your social security number.
You can't take back my knowledge.
It's time to improvise.
This debt can't have my pockets or mind.

Cause I got Melanin

There's always a debate
Discrimination due to my pigment
The Institutions made me question my Life
I didn't know if I would be auctioned off
Or behind bars or in my grave early
Because no one would accept me because of My
Melanin
In this world any day can be my LAST CALL
The government deems me to be a bad citizen
An unreliable source
But my origin reports differently
And we all have room to improve
Why attack my Melanin?
My existence is not a tragedy
But a remedy to cure hatred
Is my Melanin rubbed out of the principles to
protect and Serve?
Should I have commitment to the Constitution?
If I have no freedom
If it hurts to have a vision
Because I am being hunted and condemned
Taking for granted
Cause I got Melanin I have the Power to know the
difference
I will no longer question my being
Cause I got Melanin

Problems in a Fragmented Diary

Over a hundred words but not enough to bridge
this divide
Between these thoughts and feelings inside
I'm seeking alternative words to resolve these
issues
To strengthen my soul and love me
unconditionally
All these words but nothing seems rational
Or fit for a Queen
I guess I have to add action behind these words
To build a stronger alliance
I was blinded by words
Fooled by an illusion
I'm trying to move on
My pen has me feeling all type of ways
So, we argued about what influenced this shit
I asked my heart to revive my pen
I decided to caress my mind an anoint my energy
To reclaim the chemical performance in the
courage I once had
The power lies within
I declare freedom to allow myself to be
extraordinary
The universe called me to conquer

It Happened Within the Sun

Even though these words don't seem to be on my
side I had a weapon
I kept writing and trusting while confused on my
back
Disregarding words that wouldn't help me
conquer
I decided to caress my mind and anoint this
ordinary matter

Flesh in a Cage

Completely alone bottled with rage
Isolated from social situations; my true friend is
avoidance
Relationships has caused impairment; brutal
despair upon myself
I tried to engage and have understanding
Yet mistrust manifested in my mind
I would directly look in her eyes
Converse with her mood; hoping for greater
functioning
Trying to connect with her spiritual integrity
Yet her actions caused my heart injury
Numbing stimuli caused nights of tears
I found myself worrying often instead of letting
things flow
The lack of communication weighed heavy on my
body
Her past played in the back of my mind
Unreasonable rumors
 People didn't want us to make a connection
I silently urged for her to become my perfume
Her words triggered flashbacks
I wanted her words and actions to be in uniform
Unfortunately, detachment was left after the
ringtone

It Happened Within the Sun

When she tells me she loves me
 I figure it would bring pleasure
Instead it caused panic attacks
Stripped naked in this cage embarrassed because
I love her
Our interaction causes arousal
I want to love her I am just obligated to this damn
cage

Error

A flashback of an error,
The days when it hurt to look in the mirror
The days when I couldn't describe how I felt
I cried on my knees asking for help
Impulsive behaviors, banging my head wondering
would I be better off dead.
Damaging my spirits; being incoherent.
Not connecting with anyone thinking love wasn't
real.
Wondering if you met me, would you think I
would just become another bill.
I put up a wall, limiting my words.
Turning my emotions into a prisoner locking my
heart confining in the bars
Not accepting comments or compliments.
Feeling like kin to complaints; eyes always teary
because I didn't know my family traits.
Being distant unwilling to admit I was wrong
Thinking you never wanted me born
You weren't a part of my phases, but you caused
growing pains.
As a child, I never received a hug
As a teenager, you weren't involved in my
extracurricular activities.

It Happened Within the Sun

There isn't a picture of us that captured my
adulthood experiences.
Maybe the absence of you in my life will always
be a complicated story.
I know these eyes were inherited; whether or not
what you had with my mom was a fling.
But I know now I'm not an error because I'm able
to look in the mirror.
Yes, a little bitter but not knowing you will not
damage me.
You helped to create an artistic abstract that can
sometime be abrupt due to my life
circumstances.
However, the absence of you has strengthened
my journey.
A fatherless child with a vision,
I am able now able to be in the atmosphere of
love and learn from errors.

Mr. Chink, (Biological Father)

See I use to be the girl who felt like no one was by her side. The little girl who would cut her skin; watch the blood pour from her pores. It was a sense of relief a cry for help in times I felt defeated. I was a fatherless child who felt neglected and sometimes I didn't know how to feel. It confused my membrane. I would wonder sometimes how I let a stranger affect me so much. I mine as well place pain upon myself because I'm familiar with myself. It felt odd sometimes my brothers had their mother and father under one roof. I felt like an outcast I wanted to get out at times, I would feel disconnected. Like being on stage with no script or director somehow there was an audience.

My family tree was a mystery on my father side. The light skinned little girl with chink eyes came from, somewhere right? No visits or phone calls would you believe my DNA was up the high way a couple of exits away. Did you care who I would develop to me? Oh, I did hear about the time you did come to see me at my grandmother's house. Hello, Mr. Father Sir, who name did not appear on my birth certificate. However, I was too young to remember that attempted visit. Did you love the girl you helped to create? Abandoned from the beginning no father in sight to see my little fingers and toes. The tiny arms that one day would grow strong and she would have to hug herself. Did you wonder about the scars your absence would leave? How do I trust anyone if my own biological father neglected his responsibilities and hurt me before I could understand what hurt looked or felt like? It was like you made the wrong choice, so you just stepped aside and hope I disappeared. I felt empty but the journey now when I look back, I know it served a purpose.

Well, Mr. Father Sir. I met my siblings and I am grateful for the opportunity to now know them. I also now have your ashes. I am grateful to have a memory of you. Ashes to ashes, dust to dust. I am now able to trust I thank you for I know I was created to live in my highest self. I appreciate your absence it has amplified my ambition to live in my truest self.

Part Four: Reflections

Self-Talk

Freedom and Peace begins in your mind
Speak and Manifest Healing and Greatness
Write affirmations if needed
Turn thoughts about loving yourself into
#hashtags
If you need to see it
In order to believe it
Nothing about your Magic is untrue
There are opportunities that must wait for you
Stop being so cold with yourself
There's a light inside of you
Healing will bring warmth upon you
And surely it will display outside of you
You deserve to operate in your truest self and in
your greatest form
To live out your wildest dreams
Own your dreams and your voice
Devote your wake-ups to the nourishment of
your mind, heart, and soul
Your imperfections are okay they are welcomed
Trust yourself during the process
It may not resemble the calmness as birds in the
trees
But when it's all said and done
Being you will be a breeze
It's gon' be alright

Sun Queen

Be your own friend
This involves owning up to your shit
Be a pioneer in your Self Discovery
You can't keep running from yourself
Challenge the Stigmas
Separate the facts from the fiction
To reduce any friction
You're Beautiful
You're Divine
But still you got some shit with you
It's okay
We must address the sleep shadow in the room
Because a piece of the pie wasn't made for you
So, they think
You invented the ingredients
Strengthen yourself to take the whole damn pie
Connect your dots
It's time to eat
Accountability has to be added to your plate

Social Media Tunes

Not every post is true or even about you
One will convince you to believe
People are afraid of the truth
This is the reason people are compelled to lie on
social sites
Or post subliminally about you on social media
Speak ill on your name
Everyone deserves a hug and deserves the right
attention
See some of these people who don't like you
probably don't have a legitimate reason
They stare at you because they are looking for
something but don't know actually what
They probably don't love themselves which
seems to be a social media epidemic
People are showing themselves and it's up to us
to believe them

Mental Transactions

Keep in Mind: It's hard for some people to be themselves in society. Let people stand in their true selves. Let people grieve their traumatic events before placing a label upon them. It's ok for people to be vulnerable. Let's be more conscious of our language.

There was a time I didn't want to live. I lost my brother to a senseless act. I would sit and stare off into another galaxy. There were times when my heart skips a beat, or I felt like it wasn't beating at all. Palms sweaty days when I thought I was losing myself. I didn't want to face my reality that my brother was no longer here in the physical. Some days I wouldn't eat or bathe I was his big sister I blamed myself silently for not being able to keep him in the house the night he was killed. Flashbacks beat me down taking me back to his hospital room where he fought for his life. The conversation he and I had. All I wanted was favor and mercy to spare his life.

Furthermore, it was days and night of tears and looking for answers in a bottle which was not nourishment to my grievance. Eventually, I went to see a therapist and after the intake she went straight to prescribe me medication for depression. Ahem, I know I am depressed do you not want to know what I have been doing to cope? Can we not talk coping mechanism? So, you just want to put me on medication and not listen to what I am saying and not saying? In this case therapy didn't work for me. It was time to collect my thoughts and of course bathe and eat my love ones were worried about me. This time was beyond a dark space for me. I didn't think I would be able to manage without my bloodline. The little boy whose diapers I changed, taught to pronounce words, took care of when he didn't feel well and so much more.

I have what is called Seasonal Affective Disorder. My brother was taken from me in the winter we laid him to rest on my birthday the 14th of December. The holidays for me are a disturbance. November of 2012 was his last Thanksgiving with us, and he never made it to Christmas even though he already gave me his Christmas list. During this time, I tend to withdrawal it's hard for me to sleep. I feel hopeless at times and uncomfortable being able to still live while his life ended at 19.

Mental Health is Real and Matters

Let's gravitate towards getting the help we need.
This piece was written to escape the stigmas and
explore mental illness in urban communities.

Dear Person with a Mental Disorder, Retardation,
Mental illness, Mental Intelligence or whatever
you wish to call it.

You are a disturbance to society
The deficiency of your fabric makes us want to
scream
You are impulsive and what not, we are unable to
recognize you through your anxiety and bipolar
behavior
Your thoughts are out of control
We don't want to be bothered with your
nonsense
You are handicapped
It requires too much time
Your impairments are not beautiful
Let me tell you they are costly and a burden
With all the crazy additional expansions with
infrastructure
Access to services needs to grow because of
you...

It Happened Within the Sun

Weirdo
Why should we provide housing, jobs, and
recreation?
You can barely function
Your complexities are inappropriate for society
We don't owe you any opportunities
Think about it!
Your vision is poor; you hallucinate and hear
voices
Your mental and social capacity is low like below
the average
There's no telling what will happen when you
leave out of your house
You may feel like Jesus or be all in your feelings
all manic and psychotic
There's no way to tell
Maybe you should stay inside
No one wants to deal with your poor features
today Um. . . Let's see if there's a padded room
for you
Are you taking your meds?
How does your brain work? Or is it broken?
You make us feel so uncomfortable
Where did you come from?
You people are dangerous, hard to talk to
Some of you have a drug dependence and mixed
episodes

Sun Queen

How do you expect for people to cure you?
You are a diagnosed wreck
You want us to look at you like you're normal?
Well don't go crazy or have panic attacks
We may believe you're human, maybe

Dear Society,

I heard you were looking for me?
FUCK YOU!
Legalize my existence for I am human
I AM NORMAL!
Do not place your stigma upon me
I do not subscribe to your restraints
I did not damage society
You want me to commit suicide huh?
I won't!
I have already slit my wrist
I worked through that
I learned new coping mechanisms
I have a purpose!
I have low tolerance for assumptions
Get to know me and not my diagnosis
You do not have to treat me differently
Are you blind?
I am a person with normal intentions
I am not demonic
I am here to stay
Maybe it's you who needs some time with a
Doctor
Sounds like you need to release some things on
your mind
But me
I am Beautiful! Any Human can love me

Sun Queen

For I am not my diagnosis

Problems Pouring Out

Keep in mind our development
The strength through the stress
When you talk about that poverty-stricken
Ghetto/Hood
That place known as the slums
Where we had to cope with crisis daily
Abandoned buildings, people walking around
looking like disparity
Some days there was a shut off notice
"Where we went to the store with food stamps in
our Hand"
Not caring who was around
Those stamps would spread long
And feed the whole block if need be
That place you speak of so disgusting raised some
of us
Yea, that place where the slum lords own several
properties
Raggedy steps where we sat and did hair
Crime high
Any given day we were notified a homie from the
hood was killed
Not much silence around the way
Fights or daily raids
We continue to rise
Fuck the Inequality you placed in our streets

What do social media represent? It represents the ability to retrieve news and create anything you want and post it.

Black Needle

The Black Needle in the Room
Hurting Inside
It's interrupting what the creator has in store for
me
To truly be Divine
The rage has me acting a fool, hurting my
brothers and sisters
I'm at war with my own fist
Looking in the mirror asking for me
Are you there?
From the dysfunction of the systemic way and the
black cloud over my city
I hide in my True Self
Afraid to admit
I don't know me, I want to be loved and
understood
I barely recognize what family is
Haven't been to a reunion in a minute
I don't know the last time my immediate family
sat down together at dinner time
Shit when the sun rises
I can't even relate to the sunshine
I know I have to release my feelings though
So here I am shedding some of these feelings
A couple of verses to help you think twice

Sun Queen

There's no safe place to hide when you're trying
to live
I just want somebody to have my back
It's been a cold season that extends throughout
my historical timeline
Amerikkka guilty for the enslavement of my
ancestors, not respecting our humanity
The civil servants in blue communicating with us
Uncivilized actions
Flashing lights
Screaming disputes
Being slaughtered because of our Melanin
Tears tattooed on the walls of my people death
chambers
Flint without water is a form of depopulation
But what do I know?
To a degree I believe in conspiracy theories
Today's living is parallel to Jim Crow
We need to get in sync with our higher selves
Stop hustling backwards
Thinking peace is foreign
I get it we are scared to admit and disclose our
trauma
Figuring we'll always be a Nigga
We walk the Earth with so much pain in our
hearts

It Happened Within the Sun

The youth feeling alive and empowered because
they have access to carry a gun on their hip
Not thinking their special enough to invent
something
To live out their dreams
Throwing their hands up when they get frustrated
with a Math problem
Mama barely home to help resolve problems
She's working two and three jobs to avoid the
eviction and disconnected notices
Decision making skills isn't the hot topic on the
block
See you have to understand in some homes
Kids are raising themselves and siblings and
teaching their parents things
Oh, didn't I mention how the system tries to
leave the Black man out of our homes
Yea so not too many Fathers in the home on my
block
I must get rid of these generational scars
I believe I can change the world that's why I had
to grab my pen
And cry on my note pad
I got to release this mental slavery
The Revolution starts within me

Sun Queen

I will not be a part of a timeline where reflecting
on life is an affliction of lies and False
opportunities
These dark times can change
Shit I know longer have to visit my dad behind
bars
These days have been feeling strange
We must get it right
Understand the power of our His/Her story
BUILD yourself and your family up no matter
what.
Love yourself and Love them too
The Black Family is not paralyzed or caged to
white lies
Let's build muscles through Black Love
Pledge to know yourself
No matter how long it may take
It will take longer than a camera flash
It's like...
Swerving life through its smoke trying to figure
out my lane
Examining life through a rear-view glass
Growing through life's pain without no coupons
It's time to use more than our two eyes
We are not niggers in this raped dynasty
My neighborhood is more than a place where a
loose bogey is 50 cents

It Happened Within the Sun

Where my neighbors ask for two for $15
I do not subscribe to the white narrative
My sisters have dreams; their main focus is not
their weaves
We will Rise!
Break through the crimes, molestation, mass
incarceration, and poverty,
Gentrification
Drug and alcohol abuse
Anything that isn't healthy for the Heaven you
created in your Universe
Take time to address the Black Needle in the
Room
Admit your Trauma
Run far away from the closet of denial
The Struggle doesn't mean you lost at this Life
thing.

Standing in the Struggle

Many sleepless nights due to reflecting; The reality is we must do better and hold everyone accountable. It is our duty to spread Love and Light. Encouragement to Support and educate one another. Your voice needs to be heard your efforts are needed in your community. Not everyone can make every event it's Life! Get in where you fit in make sure your efforts travel outside of your door.

Stop kicking one another down and lend a hand to help one rise. If this fight were easy, we would have already won.
Don't give in! Keep pushing and working until we create Change!
Stop the jealousy and unnecessary bullshit it's hindering us. Learn how to come together! Learn how to reciprocate kind acts! Don't feed into the negativity surround yourself around positivity! Make a smarter decision! Give Back! You have to inner stand in order to understand! Stop typing so much and put in some action!
SHIT!

Up all Night stressed trying to decompress

It Happened Within the Sun

Took a couple of showers
Shit just to wake up in a few to punch the clock
for Massa
Thoughts everywhere
Thinking and more thinking about these lazy ass
laws
That excludes my people
I have a crush on being my own boss
We struggle but it's time for us to rise up and stay
there forever
Justice is a little messy
But We the People hold the Power
There's no restriction on us evolving
Everyone wants freedom on this journey
To experience liberty and not walk around like we
were sucker punched by the white house.
To question if we're dying from the ballots or
bullets
This shit isn't cool
But we won't walk away
Some days I wake up feeling like this shit isn't fair
To fear the narrative of the media released in the
air today
I hear the chants, Love Trumps Hate
But umm, I can't help but to be in a daze and
think of our brothers and sisters missing out on
regular days

Sun Queen

Shit don't they deserve another chance?
Back to reality with their family
Thinking there's probably a brother on the
bottom bunk sending the homie a kite asking for
The New Jim Crow
The sister learning how to do hair
Both praying their sentence isn't life
Both regularly shedding tears missing their
babies...
The sister wondering if Women rights are Human
rights
Both thought of why they weren't treated with
Humanity
Yea this shit a little messy
We can't and will not be deceived with
counterfeit truths
We are not slaves of the government
We are the Majority
Don't tuck your Royalty we descend from
Greatness
Time to build a new life
We don't deserve this Shit
So, let's give Light to the Real Emancipation
The power of the revolution cannot disappear
Shit it's Time to FIGHT BACK messy or not.

Rise Up

Every day is a struggle and a different cry
Rosa stood up while sitting down; Rosa she died
of natural causes
Emmett was lynched due to a false cause
Oh, the struggle for the people of the African
Diaspora
Jim Crow heavy hands lay upon our people's mind
Then we have Harriet who was a dreamer and a
conductor of the Underground Railroad leading
enslaved people to freedom
Malcolm X was faithful to black self defense
Oh, and brother yes America still owes Black
People for reparations
Nat turner was armed with rebellion
Tell us what we have to do to end white
supremacy?
Where do I live?
Feels like America's horror story
They assume every Black man is selling dope
Quiet about the white man or boy who plots to
shoot up the school and churches
Equality missed us
Families being torn apart sentenced to 50 years
for petty crimes
Reality is Blacks are not included in on Humanity
Stolen land

Sun Queen

Freedom isn't free
The country I live in wants to uplift the Protestant
Christians as superior and powerful
This society wants me to apologize for the color
of my skin
It's hard to sleep at night disrupted by the sirens
Worried if one of my brothers or sisters are being
pulled over and arrested for traffic stops
Then they'll lie and use their blue card and say
there's no evidence that my brothers had his
hands up and said don't shoot
We get thrown to the side and denied access
Our civil rights being violated Sunday through
Sunday
Or simply because the fear of the Black skin
Here we are still marching in the streets with a
list of demands
Pulling up seats and demanding a seat at the
table
White supremacist groups showing up in
different towns feeling privileged
Where Black bodies are murdered in the streets
A Mother tears and rage from the communities
posted on the news
Every day is a struggle, but we must take time to
celebrate Black Lives
We stand on the shoulders of greatness

Part Five: Energy

Vibing Tonight

Vibes don't lie
Wake your chakras up
Don't be afraid
Listen to the tunes in your body
Eternal peace is near
Live life in your greatest self
Enrich your everyday manifestations
Be still
Then wake your full complete self
Don't isolate your third eye
It's the highlight of your spirit insight
Today is the day to face your responsibility in the
universe
You're going to make it
Love yourself
Accept your vices they're apart of nature
You are nature
Speak to your soul
Present with transparency to move forward
You are creative
Examine your needs
Are you listening to yourself?
Nothing stays the same
Today rise and grow
Forget about the pain and confusion

It Happened Within the Sun

Water yourself so you are able to stand and grow
Stand in your strength
You are safe in your highest self
Discover mindfulness
Keep striving through your journey
Heal with your headfirst
It will shape the new transformation
To be loved by you is an adrenaline rush
Realities sometimes make you cry
It's okay get acquainted with emotions
You decided to address yourself with a
permanent relief
Of living in peace being your authentic self
Life is great when your energy is vibrant
And there are positive vibes in your spirit
Epic vibes in your artistry

Sun Queen

Let Me Love You

I'm interested in studying beyond your trauma
and pain
The world awaits your personal manifesto
Free yourself
You deserve Love
Let me receive why your smile hides from your
face
I want to capture the depth of you
To cleanse with you
Do you have a minute to listen to the music in my
pen?
I would've brought you flowers
But your elegance has my pen leaking brown
sugar
I don't know all the essentials to a Love Story
But what I do know is I want to learn the depths
of your fabric
With your abstract, sophisticated sexy self
Let me correct that
Goddess, I want to take time with your sexy mind
I hope my expressions start a revolution within
you
I'm impressed with your resistance and
commitment to change
Can you cooperate with me?

104

It Happened Within the Sun

Don't ease up on your sass; I want to show you,
you can depend on me
There isn't a need to be fearful
We will problem solve together
Black Love exist the stereotypes are weak
Your angelic substance is honey, and gold is Your
Power
I adore you for what you were created to be
I'm not asking you to be submissive
Merely, saying this will take time
Let's provide balance and persistence
My senses are activated around you
I don't have a strategic plan or anything
All I have is me
Your appearance creates passion in my eyes
And these feelings/emotions towards you
I'm subscribing to every edition of you
There's no rush in getting to know you
However, the fact remains I have a longstanding
desire to cognitively and spiritually connect to
you
To understand you past your skin
To vibrate with you in light
To add truth in your paradigm
To discover more than your Victoria Secrets
To be faithful at helping you abolishing the
darkness you once lived it

Sun Queen

It may get gloomy during this ride, but I promise
to diligently serve you
You are beyond a classical melody
You are a phenomenal blessing
To be in your presence is a privilege
Words couldn't describe your unique magical
powers
Queen you are Art
You rescue souls
My unconscious and conscious celebrate you
The way you think, walk, and speak lets me know
your Melanin is more than edible
It's worthy of believing in a love constellation
Letting you see my vulnerable side so you can
feel comfortable letting me inside

Notes in My Luggage

Note #1 To sleep with you is more than anatomy its evolution; the study of love Naked eyes smiling on my naked body. Transferring of fluids and energy this feels so good to me. The reproduction of chemistry and clarity of my dreams it appears you heard what I had to say you praise me and treat me so good. As we lay, I know dreams come true. I want your mind and soul to continue to connect with my energy

Note #2 Ashes to ashes played by mistrust; betrayed and mistreated. The love disappeared like dust. Burned by the deception; tangled by the miscommunication. I was faulted by others perception because their hidden agenda and maturity exposed them. I tried to educate them on their ignorance that blinded them. It's a shame some people think love is a game.

Note #3 I licked your lips gave you brain. I seduced your soul, now your heart is beating for me. You speak in tongue saying my name. Saying, I'm to blame for your high blood pressure". Whispering no one else can measure because you found your treasure. Together we amount to more than gold.

107

Note #4 There's something you do to me. You tried to have my mental blocked. Refusing me from wearing socks being clothed thinking I'm a hostage cutting my locs, wanting me to be bare. Not caring about my welfare. You were trying to damage my brain feeding me lies laughing while I cried. I thought you cared, you had me believing we shared common goals an interest. You asked my ring size for what so I could be the mistress. I trusted you. My mind thought it was love clearly my head was not in the correct space. So, was it lust? Yes, I know get what you can probably was your intent. You raped me strangled my reality you bruised my heart and choked my spirits. When I tried to express my feelings, you kicked me down; you did not want to hear the words I had to say. You crucified my character nailing derogatory statements in my personality. You wanted me to believe I was ugly and not worth being with you. Oh, what a shame!

You didn't understand the jewel you had in front of you. Through the process of trying to figure out what loved felt like. I had to face my reality t you and I weren't meant to be. I was too good for you; I am a good catch. I realized there wasn't a glove fit for you and me. While you're sleeping around looking for love I found love within me.

Sun's Love Trips

**There are so many reasons why I want to read
your mind.
I want to know first why you bothered to occupy
my time.
It feels like you came to destroy me.
Oh, what would I come across reading your
mind?**

Sometimes it feels like you don't know what love
is until you realize what it isn't. We all have been
in a relationship or two when after it ended, we
said to ourselves now why did I allow myself to go
through so much agony? Or what was I thinking?
Maybe times our friends and family warned us,
but we stayed anyway. Does love come and go or
is it the physical relationship that goes? It can all
be a bit confusing at times, but we have the time
to be honest with ourselves. To think with a
refreshed mindset to do what's best for our
hearts. In the beginning, flowers and cards and
your lover are your best friend.

There are relationships you thought would never
end. Feelings of amazement to have them in your
bed and most importantly they hold a special

place in your heart. The increased emotions when your partner looked you in your eyes telling you they love you, they proceed to place their lips on your forehead. Oh, the stages of relationships. Warm hearts; passionate pleasures to boiling blood questioning if you really love the person or if they can love you the way you deserve to be loved.

Aggressive arguments but secretly saying to yourself you're so damn cute when you're mad. The way their dimples deepens, or you just stare counting how their beauty marks are gracefully placed on their face. There's also those situation ships you have been in that have felt like blizzards in the summer. Then there are unfaithful days and nights. Loud laughs to louder cries, second guessing what you truly meant to the person who you thought were a perfect match for you. I can remember days I wanted to give up on relationships because I felt like at times I was suffering within the connection, losing.

Date nights to wishing they would take a permanent vacation out of my life. The rollercoaster of lust to love knowing the difference shouldn't be a steep slope; Stuck between saying yes and goodbye. I have learned so much about myself and others during these trips along my journey. For example, a ring or history will not bind souls together forever if the universe does not see fit. Everyone does not belong in your environment no matter how many times they say they will work on the relationship. Oh, and let's not forget about the times they told you they love you past life. It bruises your frontal lobe for some time. I can say there is renewal after the rocky times so trust the process and remember to love yourself during the process of unloading the luggage that is not fit for your trip.

Love isn't that difficult its people that are difficult. However, I am grateful for all the lessons, memories and the purpose that each individual served. It helped with the steps I took to move forward with understanding myself and realizing what emotions I never wanted to experience again. For example, Love doesn't manipulate you or get mad and tell you –you're fat; you will be alone forever. Remember to be obedient to your intuition whatever it looks like for you.

It Happened Within the Sun

I know it isn't right some days were nice others contaminated. The scratches turned into burns. The smiles became cries. Wounded and caged wish these feelings would go away. Strangled and bruised I don't want to be in my own shoes. This will all erase I do not lose when it comes to Love.

Relationships switch up on you so fast. Well, let me correct that people switch up on you so fast. There I was waiting for the declaration of our independence, The Unity of Our romance; the match for the candle to celebrate another chance. I'm sure there's a right road to take to endure more memories to enhance the clarity of our Love. That special feeling of our new journey; this is destiny, A high climax to intimacy.

Back to my first love where my panties don't have to come off, if I make a mistake, I can erase it, backspace, and delete it. Where my feelings aren't judged but expressed artistically to share my inner fear. My self-love and any despair. Tears may fall but my pen and paper capture it all There's no secrets no misconceptions just dedication. I don't have to worry about hear say because it only reveals what I say, writes how I feel, and displays what's real It's my paper and pen we are here to Win! Love still roams the air.

I don't mind loving me endlessly. I am transitioning to my destiny. I have evaluated the inner me. Now my love for self is deeper than you and I.

I protect my heart because what we share at times doesn't feel right. But because I love you I continue to lay with you knowing this is illegal. But the love I have for myself repeatedly plays in my soul. I would still like to kiss you everything isn't meant to be told. But honestly continue on with your true love I'll be here loving me I have romance now with my struggles because they strengthen me. Now I'll passionately kiss my flaws because they are a part of me. I can now sing a new song because I Love me endlessly.

Mental Elevation

I'll ride the waves with you
I want to kiss your inner thoughts
Consume your time with moans of intellectual
conversation
Graciously show and prove I want to grow with
you
I want you to trust me
I'm here to be your caregiver
To be the calcium for your bones
The vision of our future is breathtaking
It warms my heart
I've longed for a beautiful soul to have access to
my heart
I want to be your light
Create a stronger narrative of Love
With our energy I know will be alright
I've dreamed of intimate joys with you
Let's make this a *we* thing
Dance to our Romance
Celebrate unleashing each other scars
As we washed off one another's fears
I have love and elevation all over my skin
Let's vibe
All good things are ready to come
I know the Universe sent you
I accept

Sun Queen

I'm ready to experience the world with you
Bond and converse with you on this tour
To seduce you on all planets
This chemistry is intense and soulful
I'm comfortable with you
Come caress this naked truth
There's no rush in getting to know you
However, the fact remains I have a long-standing
desire to cognitively, spiritually and soulfully
Understand you past your skin.
I want to discover more than your Victoria
secrets.
To be faithful at being your light while we
undress your scars; Knowing in your past trauma
existed
I don't know all the essentials to a happy healthy
love story
What I do know is I want to learn the depths of
your fabric
I hope my words spark a revolution within you
I'm impressed with your competency and
commitment to change
To challenge yourself through your storms
To continuously manifest greatness
Your potential is appealing
The world waits your personal manifesto

It Happened Within the Sun

Perhaps they will understand why your smile
hides from your face
To know you reorganized your smile due to hurt
and abandonment
But surely, it's within you to deliver a smile.
Wondering if love is a battle or magical
Left with these thoughts due to broken promises
Forever didn't last a lifetime
The essence of our connection went from love to
fear
I once thought no connection would compare to
what we shared
You weren't ready so you put the blame on me
I mean you did try to ease back every now and
again
I know longer felt safe in loving you
I felt betrayed
The circle of love was ruptured
The thoughts of better days crumbled
The foundation we built was no longer solid
I need you to exhale light
My vibrations will be connected to your inhaler
It's essential for us to make it through
Let's try to find balance and make it right
Move closer I'm trying to study you
Let's become teammates strengthening our
consciousness

Sun Queen

Now this may be a struggle
I'm trying to receive a peace of mind
Daze about sweet kisses to my forehead
We hold the power to alleviate
If it gets rough- we will take a break,
Let's fall asleep in each other's arms
And the greatest reward is us in the end
I know this chemistry brings radiation to your
bones
This is our chance to grow
As well as expand the awareness of self
Let's learn more, explore the universe, and
challenge one another
This will be a fresh start within my heart
This will deepen our connection
You will look at me with pride and honor
There won't be any room for doubt
So, I'm taking this time to exchange energy
because I cherish you.
There's beauty in this journey to discover where
we are supposed to be
Let me tell you my secret....
I don't have all the answers
Or work towards being perfect
Looking forward to communicating and
compromising to have you in my life
I crave romance

It Happened Within the Sun

All I have is hope
Sometimes I'm afraid
But I have this cool feeling when I'm around you
This sensual fantasy gets me high
It vibrates pass my sleeves
Conversations linger in my soul
I'm attracted to your free spirit
Your positive ego
This feels so damn good to me
I never think about us turning on each other
Just roaming in nature
Thankful for the creator for having you cross my
path
We are no longer strangers
This was definitely not an accident
You were sent to be my solid leaf
I longed for your substance
I choose you to build this forest of consistency
See I have faith we can be a force
No more daydreaming to bring your sunshine into
my reality

Cosmic Connections

Whispers of safety when you're with this special
person
The fire that burns between the two of you gets
your attention
The things that he or she does for you,
Acknowledge your presence
Thanks for opening the door for me!
No, I haven't ate, yet
I don't have an appetite yet I'm full off your
faithfulness
I'm over here in this energy fueled by your
selflessness
No one has loved me the way you do
Spending time with you is amazing its relief from
the hidden agendas
The false sectors I once lived in
It's like you heard my outcry
When realness is present, trust is secured
My imagination now has no limit
Its peace when you connect with you twin flame
There are no longer pieces missing
Two hearts are happy
Two hearts turn into a dream of love
Two artists create a masterpiece

Prayer is a Language

Half Human
Half Goddess
For some reason at this time
I don't feel appreciated
Where do I go?
I am restless?
Where do I lay?
Dear Universe,
Show yourself to me
My smile doesn't represent me it's faded
My spirits are lazy they should be high
I don't know my name
Flowers wouldn't soothe me in this melancholy
time
Take me away remove my blindfold
I want to see and feel in a different dimension
Right now, it feels like I'm under cement
I want to rise
I am not sure how at this moment
What do you suggest I do?
I'm nervous and lost
I want to trust myself and you
Show yourself
Take me away
I admire you!
For I am here to learn from my mistakes

Sun Queen

You are the divine energy to my life's soundtrack
There's something going on inside of me
It's a bit ugly
I don't feel like your reflection
My spirit needs the laundromat
My thoughts need surgery
I must recover from this pain
Mend my insecurities and my broken heart

Colorful Lies

A broken connection
Disengaged vibes
There was a time our love was so strong
A time your presence was my peace
Our bond felt like adhesive
Loving you was a form of art
All I needed was your support
We became one without a license
Then your dark side came clear to me
You were no longer my blessing
But a nightmare
I exchanged liquid and energy with you
You forced me to go on without you
You weren't comfortable in your skin
Your logic was toxic
I don't know how you sleep at night
Knowing the damage, you did
Pretending to love me
You never wanted me to adjust my crown at the
altar with you
There was a time you were humble
Then you started playing tricks with my heart
It seemed like you started to hate me because
you were still figuring yourself out
Conversations became weakened and weird

Sun Queen

Honesty, there were times I didn't want to pick
up the phone
I did it because I didn't want to miss a beat
speaking to you, wanting to know about how
your day went
Your motive was only to fed me lies
I fell in love with the colorful lies
You told me it was about you and me
You would speak about how our future would be
Love, traveling, a garden and so much more
Not to mention while doing this our last names
would have changed
The truth hit the canvass it displayed you weren't
ready to put in work
I'm not sure what happened but things between
us were detaching from the sweet chemistry that
once sparked our bodies
The tension in the air was like a deadly disease
It wasn't fair how you carried me along the
invisible line
But now I see you weren't meant for me.

Heal the Heart & Mend the Mind

Forgive my treatment and generational hurt that lingers in your body and mind. Forgiving your lower self will enhance your ability to evolve. Healing is an ingredient for happiness and being healthy. It restores your thoughts and feelings of bondage. When you heal it also helps to restore your heart and soul. You can't fake it. The pain you been through that lead to adult trauma seems to be following you.

Take a minute to breathe imagine you are in a healing circle. Flowers and bubbles are on a big screen. You're sitting in a peaceful society; can you smell the incense and sage burning? Smells like Lemongrass and lavender. Sit with your thoughts everything shared here is confidential. Lay back. Here in this society you are able to get your hair, hands, and feet washed free if you are open to the services. Wouldn't it feel good to have your temples massaged? A booked session just for you all expenses paid your skin being oiled; while your frustrations are being rubbed out. Here you can relax and grow through what caused conflict upon you. However, I will challenge you to listen beyond what your ears

125

receive. To see beyond your two eyes; to be guided by spiritual company to create a sensual and sensible atmosphere that will allow you to break cycles. For great energy and understanding will transfer unto you. No blockages, working on the betterment of self.

Taking steps toward healing is restoring your voice and power. It isn't easy but it definitely can be done when you are not blinded and choose to build your internal equity. It allows you to transform into your truth.

The moment you fall into your own arms and heal the thunder and lightning will not scare you as much. You will realize it's necessary for the clouds to collide. You will be able to connect and soon feel liberated from the touch of yourself. Celebrate your struggle for it was the trials and tribulations that empowered you to notice your beauty.

Yea, I know you can't believe some of things happened to you but honestly those were the best parts of your life that was meant for you. For you go through and grow through. The scars left symbolize the strength in you. For you are here to

126

look at your scars and know they did not scare
you away from your destiny.

For your resilience is the superhero energy within
you. Sometimes you feel like you been here
before or a stranger in your own world, huh?
Sometimes you have to have patience and listen
to the wind beside you. Listen to the rhythm of
your heart.

Look at yourself long enough to be able to
identify and address your fantasy and reality. Sit
for a moment and think about how you felt when
you father never came to bring you to the park.

It's probably easier to isolate yourself, to not deal
with issues that may have been problematic for
you at some time. Authorize yourself to disclose
all information needed regarding your healing.
This will be a process; you may feel angry,
frustrated, overwhelmed and lonely. Yet you will
be the one who will be able to show up and
present in your true self. You do not have to hide
in make-up or let your moods affect your
relationships.

Now you will be able to determine what truly is upsetting you and causing you to react in such a manner that does not reflect who you are. This will help you to continue to grow from your past experiences. Be mindful of your triggers the pressure of pain feels the same the same no matter who caused it or what year it happened. It's up to you to react to what is present and not what the situation reminds you of. The healing process is the birth of your true self. Lay to rest your reckless dysfunctional behavior, thoughts of killing yourself, Destroy your lower self.

No more feelings of yourself being a pathetic human. People in life will judge you most of the time it takes the pressure off them to dealing with their own insecurities and fears. Keep in mind you are here to make yourself and space a better place for you. Mistakes are another form of second chances learn from the experience and correct it. You control your life do not give others the power to control you. There are benefits of making your soul feel good by understanding your pain. Set aside time to be present, be aware of your breathing. Are you taking deep breaths? I know you're tired of being strong and feel drained from things that have compromised your wellness. Hang in there everything is for a reason. Trust the universe to find peace in strenuous times. Dysfunction will not rule all the days of your life.

Your true self wouldn't fit on a canvass, which is fine because you would limit yourself. Reveal what makes you not support yourself. Was it someone in your past that didn't believe in you or told you, you wouldn't amount to anything? It appears you hold some resentment with someone in your past that is holding space in your present. You do not have to keep things at a surface level. A deeper level may bring you to tears and weak muscles. However, I am sure you are making room for productivity, and your well being. Be vulnerable and authentically you.

Apologize and forgive for all the cold winters you experienced in June. Apologize to yourself for beating yourself up and self-medicating instead of self-loving because you felt like you were a mistake. Apologize and forgive yourself for drowning in that abusive relationship you stayed in because you didn't know what true love looked or felt like. Hey, you may have been told you were a fool if you left because of their salary and

129

or the materialistic things he or she beat you up with. To cover the insecurities and the fact they weren't for you. Yes, another family secret. There probably were days you wanted to jump from the lack of attention and love in your home. Please know that you are beautiful and loved the Universe would never deny or disown you. Forgive your mother, the school activities she missed. Forgive for all the times you needed hugs and encouraging words and she told you to go in your room. See momma could have grown up in a home that was not very expressive where affection was a sign of weakness. Momma could have been told chin up girl one day you will have to provide and work hard there isn't any time to be all up in your feelings. It's a cold world out there and you have to be prepared for life. Who knows momma's struggle? Forgive Momma for not believing you when you told her you were raped. She more than likely believed you and did not know how to deal with the pain. She had thoughts of failing, as a mother sleeping for her wasn't the same after you told her this. She wanted to kill the monster that took advantage of her baby girl. She didn't know how to express her feelings. She wanted to tell the authorities it's she grew up in a home where what was shared stayed between the family and in the home. You couldn't go telling outsiders family business.

Forgive your father for the neglect. You managed to blossom without him directly affecting your days. He didn't make a mistake having you. Becoming a father to many was a continued learning experience for him.

We are human and unfortunately but fortunately there will be uncomfortable times in our lives. We must learn from the things we put out in the universe.

Part Six: Tiger's Eye

Magnificent One

You are not the minority and cannot be
duplicated.
Grow and mature in your DNA.
Suffering produces Queens and Kings.
I know some days life can be described as a
demon.
There's a Purpose!
Hold On!
Understand you have the qualifications to create
a new light.
Lead yourself and your people out of darkness.
There is a beginning and an end.
However, throughout the struggle never give up.
I know it can be frustrating and you feel you tried
your best.
Acknowledge your bloodline and keep fighting.
Your freedom and justice are near.
Take a moment to get closer to you.
It isn't so far to go.
It's not about following the trend.
Or being a slave to the enemy.
It's about being intimate with your True self.
Believing and receiving all inspiring
manifestations.
Moving in a Divine Manner

Sun Queen

Trusting yourself to empower and inspire yourself
and the rest of your people.
Souls are eternal
Make your contribution to the Universe
breathtaking and noble.
Your legacy will be an interpretation of you.
You are not a disabled being.
You are a part of a revolutionary magical solar
system.
You are the Liberator!
Be faithful to your change process.
Give it all You Got!
I am not saying it will be easy.
You may want to shout of frustration due to the
sounds of violence and the constant struggle to
stay alive.
Or be in enraged because of the corrupted
systems.
Or riot because of the inhumane responses from
the administration.
It may appear there's so much friction.
Worst has become the worst
Know the youth will flourish, things will shift.
Don't rethink your experience
Create hope in the renewal of you being the
change with the Science.

Suffering and the struggle will come in this
secular matrix shit.
Resist!
Your strength won't go out of style.

Black Wombman

Her zest takes the rain away
How can you deny her sensation and ability?
Look deeper into her eyes
The resilience is true
Hold her she carries the world on her shoulders
Her frequency is stronger than sperm
Her ability is more than warming bottles of
Enfamil or Similac in the middle of the night
She's Nubian
She's' Black
She's just Dope like that
Get you a Black Wombman
She will make your life better
A Black Wombman is not a mystery
She's more than a fat ass and thick hips
Her nurturing spirit wasn't created to just be a
caregiver for Tom's children
She will not break; don't rob her from her awards
She is the Universe, don't judge her assuming the
Black Wombman is just mean
She is the gasoline for the vehicle to journey
through life
Don't delete her feelings. . . Her emotions
She is the alarm clock to wake you up
She doesn't have to make you want her

It Happened Within the Sun

She's a Beauty Queen
You just will... in the grand scheme of things
She is just the enlightenment that your soul
needs
Freedom and Peace unto your mind
Deeper than a Religion
Get Baptized in The Black Wombman
You'll never find another quite like her
Within her is nature, the sky, beauty, and the
Universe
The Black Wombman is a Blessing
The beginning of Life
The Black Wombman is Art
Her existence and shape is divine craft
She wasn't created to work for you
Fuck white supremacy
White privilege and all the other nonsense
You cannot wake up and be The Black Wombman
Ha, all the surgeries are a waste
By the way you never thanked my ancestors for
taking care of little Charlie
The Black Wombman is just her
Africa is in her DNA
Don't act like you'll aren't aware of her DNA
The Black Wombman genetic traits go back to the
oldest human skeletal remains
The birth of the human race

Sun Queen

She will always make it out of the rain
Stress couldn't keep her down
Pain has lifted her energy in so many ways
Providing for her family and society
Her melanin cannot be mistaken
She will never settle
She knows she's a Queen
The Black Wombman is destined to rise
She is unapologetic is her substance and tone
The Black Wombman provides light of ten
thousand suns
This got to be Heaven
Being merry next to a Black Wombman made out
of brown sugar, honey and cocoa
The fire inside a Black Wombman will keep you
warm
What's better than the Black Wombman
She will help you produce wealth
Be ready for your Black Wombman
Love her
Explore with her
Reach your destination with her
Shoot pass the Moon
Love a Black Wombman
It's time to conquer the world
Hold her tight
Don't let her out of your sight you need her.

A Radical in the Water

Where are the instructions or the manual for this
Fight?
Sometimes I feel stuck surrounded by gorilla
tape.
In my spare time, often I can be found under a
tree manifesting
UNITY
Reciting over and over Peace and Justice will be
declared
No more Black bodies in the streets
Shit!
There's way more to the struggle than the fight
against the Police and their terrorism.
Things are barely done out of love anymore.
The Government and the Trump Administration
ad-ministering all types of poisons, laws, bigotry
and budget cuts
To keep us from pressing forward.
It's hard to hold down a household off of ten
dollars and ten cents.
Never mind trying to paint a healthy picture
without medical insurance.
How do I make healthy goals and set boundaries?
We are living in times where it's getting hard to
separate the poor from the working class.
No pun intended

Sun Queen

A career after college with decent figures isn't
guaranteed.
But what is?
The fragrance of the struggle
It continues
It'll be a long time but I'm here to heal and right
some wrongs
To help feed my people
Restore our communities
I am a verb
I am the Sun
I shine
I am an Icon
I will find my way I'm here to support
Background chatter and closed doors won't stop
me.
I am here to move beyond the surface.
Not here to be like anyone
Just evolve in my organic self.
I may not look or sound like your average
organizer or activist.
Wait scratch that title shit
I'm me
That doesn't matter though
It's what's in my heart
And I can careless who likes me
Just don't address me with the negativity

It Happened Within the Sun

This isn't a facade it's my passion and a layer of
me
See I want to do more than put my city on the
map
I want to teach the youth how to plant seeds
And what steps to take to nurture them and
watch them grow
I'm not here to beat the system
I am here to be a part of dismantling the system
I will hold myself accountable while holding city
officials accountable too
I won't lie; sometimes this life and fight to survive
will make you want to run
There are organizers and activist or whatever
name one prefers.
With a thousand thoughts and no strategic long-
term plans.
Ego's overpowering thought; craving the limelight
crashing the work.
Reducing the positive progress
See there's no Gold shining, Grammy, with this
work and you should be fine
Your work may not get the Best Service of The
Year Award.
It isn't about five stars or thousands of followers
on your Facebook page.
This movement wasn't built for the fame.

Sun Queen

You may not get grants or overflowing donations.
What you gon' do?
In a room of fighters, you never know who's your
comrade or enemy.
Wondering who will be the monster to hold the
gun up to your vision.
The shackles moved from our feet to our heads.
Our brains have us moving backwards.
Not working effectively and collectively.
Solidarity has to be explained.
People will pull up to scene to be seen just for the
cameras.
Our people need us after Channel 8 and The
Independent News leave.
Everyone's mission and vision are different.
Yes, but we have to move on
On one accord; with the mindset of the common
denominator, and for The Liberation of our
people.
I get it though
There are so many broken people trying to
change broken
Amerikkka.
It starts within.
In all we do
We possess greatness in our DNA

Yes, but let's be real there's also generational
hurt and pain.
Let's heal to crack these broken codes.
Here we are doing work with the intentions of
revolutionary Malcolm philosophies and wanting
Martin's dream to become reality.
Moving with empty cups
Acting like we don't have common sense in our
pockets.
We must heal ourselves before we start singing
like Michael to heal the World.
Let us not be dangerously dysfunctional
But UNAPOLOGETIC and Fearless

Letter to my Brother

Dear Chris,
The portrait of our family will now reflect a
bruised expression. This pain is brutal; these
emotions hard to balance. How will your Big
sister ever function in accordance? Liquid tears
now pour from my eyes through my veins the
word competence is voided during this difficult
time, a senseless person took what was and is
mine. You will remain my baby boy; I taught you
how to spell your name and constantly
played games with you. The memories of you will
comfort me and our family. Your smile is planted
in my bones.

This tragedy has tormented my brain; a sister left
insane "Mush" in spite of it all I will remain your
big sister and advocate. No institution or
community could ever describe your built or
frame; nor share your story. I pray we get to
experience new land together, until then please
be my safeguard. It's more than hard to put
words together to express the love and bond we
share. I will never say goodbye; your spirit
is formatted in the element of my being. With
this being said, "Mush" I respect and salute you

for your relevancy in my life. My soldier little
brother who always wanted chicken nuggets
when he was younger. Cheers to your life the
conclusion will never make sense. In our words
"you ugly yo" I hope all these words translate to I
Love You, our last verbal words SAFETY; I LOVE
YOU! While you were fighting to remain in the
physical, I prayed and asked for favor and mercy
to be granted.

 I guess this is what it looks like your assignment
here was complete. It surely doesn't feel like it.
But Mush, it's been 5 weary years since your
body left this Earth. There hasn't been
any evidence of the cruelty done to you.
Often times, when I stand at your resting spot, I
hear you say don't worry I'm good.

As your big sister eye feel like eye owe it to you,
to seek Justice Anger often times flows from my
heart because your murder is still unsolved. Boys
in Blue claim they are working; but nothing.

Maybe they need to put in overtime or maybe
they don't care about the Black body that
murdered your black body I am no detective but
what I uncovered is that eye must remain hopeful

for peace and know your spirit remains. The circle of light in the sky represents you. I smile because you are my sunshine. My days go up and down, but I am forever grateful for the sprinkle of your 19 years. I will always shed tears our bond was a gift. Who else made you the best chicken nuggets? Remember when you started making eggs in the microwave? Oh, the memories we have.

Rest in Power ♛Chris

Dear Mama,

I love you!

I write this letter with gratitude and endearment. Thank you for giving me life yes, I know you brought me into this world and could take me out at any moment. Oh, the small joys of having a black mother. The things they would say to you when you were younger that didn't have real meaning until you began to understand life. Or you would say things like I don't care if you get mad, I'm your mother you are not mine. Ma, you have been my resource center in my life. You have sacrificed so much for me.

I know growing up at times I could be unpredictable, bratty, angry, and let my teenage mood swings control me. I'm sorry for all the doors I slammed and the words I mumbled under my breath and for the times I sucked my teeth. Thank you for not knocking my eyes or teeth out. You definitely had patience and didn't hold any of my childish ways against me.

Looking back, you may have not come to everything I was involved in. Or told me you love me often, as I wanted to hear. That it could have

147

been a generational trait not sure. I am proud of how many times you tell my niece and nephew you love them. If it was generational cycle look ma, you broke it. You didn't force me to participate in anything I did not have a passion for. You let me make choices and allowed me to be free spirited. I do know every time I crossed a stage you were there proud. I received my acceptance letter to my 1st school of choice; you were so excited you told the world. I also understand now as an adult even though we hope to attend everything and be everywhere we cannot. We can do what we can and make the best of what we have.

You have been my grocery store, hotel, doctor and so much more. No one has made chicken stretch the way you did growing up. It was a blessing to eat every night but Ma why chicken? (Smile). Nothing can take away the love I have for my Mama. You showed me the importance of hard work and how to climb mountains without boots if I needed to. With a minimum wage paycheck and subsidies, you always provided the necessities and fulfilled our wants.

It Happened Within the Sun

Ma, you lived in your truth and opened my eyes to so much as a child you made it clear for me to always be no matter what others may think of me. People will always judge and have an opinion, but it was not my responsibility to worry about people's views for their views did not concern me I can remember being so nervous about sharing my sexual preference. I than realize I shouldn't be, and I only cared out sharing with you and how you felt. You responded with I love you and that's that is who you are its okay.

Whew when your mama accepts you for loving the same sex. Society will slander you and believe you are ill. However, it was in her womb I was created. You did not question what you did wrong as a parent. I heard some harsh coming out stories where people were disowned and treated poorly by their family. It is unfortunate one would have to go through so much strife with sharing their truth. I thank you mama for helping me walk in my life and loving me through it all. I know I am probably your wild radical child in a different light because we all had our wild moments.

Sun Queen

It was the way you supported and helped anyone that came through your door that needed help that you inspired me to join the movement. You showed me that we must help each other in life and take care of one another because we are all we got. When I was planning to start Black Lives Matter New Haven with my friend's memories of all your good deeds came before me. When we host community drives you are the first one to donate and spread the word. For I am your child and I knew I had to give back to my community and fight for our people. For life is worth fighting for and you showed me through standing tall through life's adversities.

You tried your hardest to not show my brother's and I your struggles but I'm nosey remember I am your child. Who knows more than you? Speaking to you is better than watching the news. I ear hustled and peeped my little eyes through doors. You lifted yourself out of addiction and abuse. There have been times I wondered how in the midst of storms you had peace. You are brave and I wouldn't change anything about my childhood as it has shaped me to be who I am today. I now appreciate all the time I had to babysit my brothers for our bond is unbreakable.

It Happened Within the Sun

Thank you for all you have done for our family for
you embody Love and Kindness.

I appreciate you! For I don't live in fear I live in
my truth.
Because of you I am me;
Because of you I can because of you I will
Because of you I will break cycles
Because of you I know how to grow through
struggles
Because of you I know how to season chicken just
right; I never mastered the diabetic Kool- Aid
Because of you I will never be ashamed of my
identity
Because of you I know how important it is to keep
a clean house even if I just cleaned up ten
minutes ago
Because of you I value myself; I am unapologetic
Because of you I know to always smile and fight
even if I feel like I am drowning
Because of you I open my door to all those in
need I provide an ear even when I have my own
things going on but it does not stop me from
being present for others
Because of you I give and give and give you
could've spared me that trait (Smile)
Because of you I smile at adversity

Sun Queen

Mama in you I trust!

Dear Tomi Veale,

Once upon a time, I met someone who cared about a young girl who wasn't always satisfied with how things went on in her life. Thank you for being you; now I strive to be the best me. You are selfless and inspire me.

L. E. A. P was a summer home for neighborhood kids including me. It was a safe, happy, fun and a learning place; which orchestrated positivity and development for the youth. I still as an adult start my day with daily affirmations. In L. E. A. P, we went on long journey trips out of state which allowed me to see there was more to the world than New Haven, CT. Camping also had a positive impact on me. It helped me to connect with nature and the stars, to spend time with the Sun.

Camping introduced me to the Universe at an early age. It was a different element to learn how to navigate through life. The program was a child's paradise with so many activities, fundraisers, and snacks. A community to increase learning, I was blessed to have you as a counselor you believed in me. A young girl with a teenage attitude, you committed to helping the young girls in the "hood" to develop skills.

153

Dear Ms. Onya Harris,

For I was not a case study, you saw the best in me.

You were placed in my life for a reason and have made an impact on my life. When I met you, I was angry, broken and felt helpless. Thank you first of all for accepting me and loving me for exactly who I am. Thank you! Because of you I attended the same HBCU you graduated from. I must say which one of the best experiences in my life.

For it was you that assisted with rescuing me, you helped me understand myself. You were one of the first people to help me identify my feelings. You taught me so many awesome things especially during the times when I felt so alone. You give great and genuine advice. You helped me realize speaking with a therapist was not necessarily about a diagnosis. You helped me face my struggles in a positive light. You introduced me to coping mechanisms.

You were always available. You never gave up on me. You challenged me. You listened to my problems I presented and the ones I kept in side. When I didn't want to talk nor able to use my words to express my confusion you would let me play a game or sit in silence. I have cried, screamed, cursed in your space. I also felt safe and comfortable with you.

To this day I have not found a therapist like you. I guess because you were more than a therapist. In my head you were Auntie Onya. I was eager to overcome my trials and I found a great place, your office. For it was your office where I realized I could smile putting forth the effort to think things through and make changes. The world needs more people like you.

We outlined the things in my life that had my brain doing flips. You have been there for my highs and lows my relationship wows and whys. You rode the wave with me after I left your office. When you see me now, I can tell by the excitement in your eyes you are reflecting on how far I've come. Our conversations are always rejuvenating; you lift my worries from shoulders.

You advocated for me. For you reminded me my life was worth it and I could turn things around for me, I should live it to the fullest. You also helped me to realize I am bigger than the world I live in and I can create magic anywhere I go as long as I work hard for what I want. You always pushed me to be the best version of myself. You let me know I had potential to be a leader.

Thank you for talking me through all my life encounters.

Dear Angela Y. Davis,

A woman who speaks truth to power, thank you for addressing problematic issues; inappropriate, and offensive. Things of this nature do not liberate society. I celebrate you; for you are a black woman, an activist, author, and educator your work is truly admired. You have used your voice for marginalized people, and the reflection of your work is intellectual content for me. Thanks to you I want to be able to improve the opportunities for black lives whom face so many disparities.

It feels good to see strong successful women who look like me. My path is design for me, but I am thankful for you have been a distant but close mentor in the streets, media, and books and of course in my head. I had to learn emancipation of self before I could comprehend social emancipation. Your courage and love for the liberation for people inspires me. You always stood your ground never afraid to resist.

You are a gentle militant woman much honor belongs to you. You are such a divine civil rights icon. You moved my mind for the path to fight for justice. The time is now to lace up my boots and

157

fight. I want to clear my energy so I can receive my full purpose in this fight. I wish for you to take me in under light to help me prepare for the days that have yet to come in the struggle. What a pleasure it would be to learn from a great example.

A young girl growing up in a cold world I knew I had to end up in a higher institution than be in bondage in a prison institution. Your book Freedom Is A Constant Struggle was written with knowledge and wisdom. I have listened to you speak in New York at the Kaufman Music Center and Afro Punk. I wish I could be at every venue you are present. To listen to your truth; your break down on why we need to make connections globally. As you say we all are neighbors, with thinking this way it would allow us to diversify the movement. Every time I've heard you speak you always pay homage, and you lift up the Black Women who have come before us and pay respect to the ones who are presently fighting for justice. This is important for us to acknowledge that there is a long list of black women who are and were courageous. This let woman in my generation know to keep fighting

It Happened Within the Sun

for human liberation. To keep moving in the right direction and we will be all right.

I lost my youngest brother; he was 19 years old, due to gun violence. Before that he spent 5 years as an inmate number in the system. I understood the truth about the school to prison pipeline; slavery behind bars.

> *Radical simply means, "grasping things at the root. ~Angela Davis*

When I began researching your legendary and revolutionary work it was like a sermon my soul needed. I was in the beginning process of understanding the power of my consciousness. I was living in a moment I wanted to align my mind, body, and soul. While doing this I was eager to stand tall and walk as rebel but learning so much about your work and journey. I have a deeper understanding of the term and dedication to the word radical. I wanted my essence to be a silhouette of Black Power this was my time take control of my own learning of Black History.

For me this means to be hungry for the need of change to interconnect the roots to the problem that we may nourish our lives through manifesting freedom. You planted these words to speak to me that I may push through the deception to understand the problem while subscribing to the full truth that will stand next to the solutions. This implies to study the history of racism to break through the spirits of oppression and other isms. Not to live in restraints but to stand up and speak out.

Your courage and love for the liberation for people inspired me.

You courageously affirmed our Human Rights matter. You eloquently explain frameworks vividly describing pain and injustice. While speaking you comforted me with your humble posture and energy. The way you pour the need for a revolution gives me power within me. I hope when the Revolution reaches under the sun you will be aside me to hold my hand. You remind me it will be all right if we educate ourselves and continue to fight starting at the root of the problems. We must not get comfortable and be at a standstill because this our daily lives is a constant struggle and the cycles must come to an end. It is time to free our minds from the tainted transmitted lies of society.

Thank you for being a role model. You inspire me to stand my ground on issues that are important to me. I appreciate and value everything I have learned from you. It will forever remain a major part of history and the movement for liberation. I look forward to the day I can be a highlight in someone's life and history.

About Sun Queen

Sun Queen writes poetry, she is known for her activism.

Sun Queen is a student of the universe and life's elements. She is one of the co-founders of Black Lives Matter New Haven. Sun has been in the helping profession for over 10 years. She is committed to advocacy and inspiring people it has always been a passion for Sun. Her passion and love for advocating grew extensively after the traumatic loss of her brother Christopher Fain, a 2012 New Haven homicide victim whose case has not been solved to date. Sun has provided helping services with an array of professional titles; she is an artist and inspirational messenger.

Sun's artistry is a reflection of life through her lenses, which sparked her third eye to awaken. She vowed to cultivate her being by presenting in her organic and authentic self. Through advocating and guidance, she has helped people, who didn't think it was possible to elevate and

162

understand, life's journey by sharing her narrative and appreciating her struggle.

Sun Queen is one of the co-founders of Black Lives Matter New Haven established in 2015. BLM New Haven's mission is to demonstrate integrity through educating individuals of all ages while helping increase their knowledge on Laws as well as their individual rights. BLM New Haven's goals are solely to inspire and empower the community through Advocacy, Education, and community service, in order to create long-lasting solutions to social problems. We envision reforming our community, emphasizing on accountability, discovering new knowledge, and sharing our resources with the community. Doing so will allow BLMNH to recognize the strength of our community, encourage education and inclusion on community matters to promote change and growth.

Sun Queen strives daily to expand community services and offerings to the New Haven community in which she was born and raised and resides until this present day. For the past couple of years, Sun Queen has organized Back to School Drives in which several dozens of backpacks and school supplies are provided to families that may be in a financial bind or families truly in need as well as a Homeless initiative which provides toiletry care packages to homeless residents of New Haven. Sun Queen is a student of the universe and life's elements. Sun has been in the helping profession for more than 10 years, she is committed to advocacy and inspiring people, which has always been a passion of hers. Her passion and love for advocating grew extensively after the traumatic loss of her brother Christopher Fain, who is a 2012 New Haven homicide victim whose case has still not been solved to date. Sun has provided helping services with an array of professional titles. She has participated in a host of events within her community which has allowed her to volunteer, including but not limited to; community marches, rallies, and even fundraising campaigns geared at empowering and educating the young and older community of their rights using nonviolent principles.

Sun is a poet, an artist, and an inspirational messenger. On a daily basis you can find Sun on social media and in real life being nothing but pure and true to her authentic self. Sun Queen is currently in the process of writing and self-publishing a book of poetry. Many have described her work as "beautifully capturing with divine insight." Through her passion and love for advocacy and guidance, she plans to help others be able to share their stories.

Overall, Sun Queen's vision is to create a safe and vibrant space that will bring truth to power; allow her to also interconnect the roots to the problem that we as individuals may use as nourishment in our lives in order to be able to manifest our freedom. Sun's goal is to create a space where Women of Color will able to go and build confidence; all while focusing on personal wellness maintenance. Her wishes for the people in her community are to have individuals be open to healing and the understanding of trauma and self-love. She feels as if this will be a step towards liberation and becoming intimate with your true infinite self. Sun believes that with unity, a strong community support system will be achieved.